THE
DUFFER'S
GUIDE TO
GETTING MARRIED

COLUMBUS BOOKS
LONDON

Other books in the Duffer's series:

The Duffer's Guide to Golf: A Second Slice (Gren)
The Duffer's Guide to Rugby (Gren)
The Duffer's Guide to Coarse Fishing (Mike Gordon)
The Duffer's Guide to Cricket (Gren)
The Duffer's Guide to Booze (Gren)
The Duffer's Guide to Rugby: Yet Another Try (Gren)
The Duffer's Guide to Snooker (Mike Gordon)
The Duffer's Guide to D-I-Y (Mike Gordon)
The Duffer's Guide to Skiing (John Fairbanks)
The Duffer's Guide to Football (Gren)
The Duffer's Guide to Horse-racing (Mike Gordon)
The Duffer's Guide to Staying Married (Gren)
The Duffer's Guide to Electioneering (Gren)
The Duffer's Guide to Horse-riding (Gren)
The Duffer's Guide to Squash (Mike Gordon)

First published in Great Britain in 1986 by
Columbus Books Limited
19–23 Ludgate Hill, London EC4M 7PD
Reprinted 1986, 1987, 1988

Typeset by Cylinder Typesetting Limited,
85A Marchmont Street, London WC1N 1AL

Printed and bound in Great Britain by
Redwood Burn Limited, Trowbridge, Wiltshire

ISBN 0 86287 269 3

CONTENTS

Introduction: 5
Finding a Partner: 6
Which girl shall I marry?
  The raving beauty
  The good-time girl
  The cooking fanatic
  The athlete
  The motherly type
  The highly intelligent career woman
Which man shall I marry?
  The disco kid
  The romantic
  The company man
  The poseur
  The sugar daddy
  The academic
How to Meet Members of the Opposite Sex: 19
  The dance
  Join a club
  Advertise
  Computer dating
How to Propose: 24
Getting Parents' Approval: 30
Deciding upon the Day: 32

Choosing the Ring: 35
  Advice to the bride
  Advice to the groom
The Guest List: 38
Where Shall We Hold the Wedding?: 39
  The cathedral
  The church
  The country chapel
  The register office
The Wedding-present List: 44
Hiring Suits: 45
The Stag Party: 46
The Hen Party: 47
The Bridal Carriage: 48
The Bride's Bouquet: 49
The Wedding Day: 50
  The best man
  The bridesmaids
  The ushers
  Confetti
  The wedding photographs
The Reception: 56
  The posh 'do'
  Stylish, but not over-expensive
  The small, select dinner
  The family thrash
  The seating plan

Who Does What at the Reception: 62
  The best man
  The bride's father
  The groom's father
  The groom
A Day to Remember: 67
Understanding Wedding-day Jargon: 68
The Wedding Night: 73

4

Introduction

Are you considering whether to get married? Are you considering getting married provided you can find someone who will marry you? Either way, you will want the big day to go without a hitch.

Nothing is more likely to cast a cloud over the day than to arrive at the church (having just discovered you've forgotten to order the cake) to find that the vicar has left for a golfing holiday with the organist.

So, dear reader, read on. Take heed of our advice on planning your wedding day. By so doing, you can guard against many of the common pitfalls.

Finding a Partner

Just because you've decided to marry, it must not be assumed that you have, at this stage, anyone *to* marry. We at Duffer's Guide Headquarters (nothing if not thorough) will therefore now assess various types of the opposite sex you may find worthy of consideration as your prospective bride or groom.

Which girl shall I marry?

1. The raving beauty

Never marry a raving beauty. She will spend all her time grooming herself. Any amorous advances will be repelled with the words, 'Stop it, you're ruining my make-up'.

Any suggestion that she should do something creative in the kitchen will be laughed at because domestic activity of that kind could ruin her nails.

Never marry a raving beauty.

2. The good-time girl

Never marry a good-time girl, either – you'll be worn out within a month of meeting her and she won't slow down just because you've put a ring on her finger.

After a hard day at the office, she'll expect you to be swinging by 6.30, mixing your cocktails or gins-and-tonics for another wild night, which ends at dawn with drinks at friends' houses.

She can't understand why you, crawling to work at 9 am, aren't excitedly looking forward to the thrash she's lined up for that evening.

Good-time girls are for dating, not marrying.

3. The cooking fanatic

Never marry a fanatical cook: she'll be so busy feeding you with her latest calorie-packed offering that within a year you'll be a fat, shambling pudding of a man whose ambitions, sex-drive and sporting aspirations have been swamped by her gastronomic adventures.

Never marry a cooking fanatic. She'll kill you.

4. The athlete

Never marry an athlete. Athletes all smell of liniment and normal, lustful suggestions on the subject of conjugal rights will never be compatible with vigorous training schedules.

The meals athletes throw together are pretty uninspiring, too. Who can get excited about a candle-lit dinner for two when it consists of bran cake and multivitamins?

Never marry an athlete.

5. The motherly type

Never marry the motherly type. The house will always be full of kids (one or two of them yours). She'll be inventing games for them, taking them on outings or reading stories to them, while you — starving after a hard day at the factory — will be forced to eat runny jelly and blancmange left over from someone's birthday party.

Never marry the motherly type.

6. The highly intelligent career woman

This one's not for marrying, either. You'll find yourself at home doing the housework while she's abroad somewhere cementing a multi-million pound deal.

Her idea of a romantic evening is sipping pink champagne in bed with the *Financial Times* and a few trade magazines.

Never marry this type.

In fact, maybe you ought to find someone all by yourself without our help.

12

Which man shall I marry?

1. The disco kid

Never marry a disco kid. He may look great gyrating under the flashing disco lights, but by the time you get him up the aisle his gymnastics will have ruined his discs and for the rest of your married life you'll hear, 'Wot, *me*? Me lift the bins out? Me wiv me dodgy back? You've 'ad it, girl.'

Never marry a disco kid.

2. The romantic

The romantic will soon drive .you mad; he'll remember all your special little anniversaries when it's obvious to all that you've forgotten them.

Even the romantic, candle-lit dinners for two will become wearing. And if you've just settled down in curlers, old nightie and comfy slippers in front of the telly with a cup of tea, it's unnerving to see friends leaping out of cupboards, from behind curtains and through patio doors as your romantic husband cries, 'Surprise, surprise, darling! It was ten years ago today we first met, remember?'

Never marry a romantic.

14

3. The company man

Never marry this type. You will just become his chauffeur and unpaid secretary. If you look decorative enough, he may invite you to some deal-clinching dinner in the hope that you can distract his customer from reading the small print in the contract for so long that he'll sign anything to avoid looking silly.

Never marry the company man – you'll be filed under W for Wife or W for Who?

4. The poseur

Never marry a poseur. He may look good in a smart bar or on a yacht but he'll get on your nerves – wearing out all your mirrors with his incessant preening.

It's very irritating, too, to find that his make-up takes up as much room as yours on your dressing-table. Worst of all, even if you have spent all day making yourself look good for that special night out, he'll still look better than you.

Never marry a poseur.

5. The sugar daddy

Never marry a sugar daddy. He may have been great as a sugar daddy, but as a husband he'll be a dead loss.

All his charm will dissolve when you see him without his wallet, and when you first wake up to the sight of his smiling teeth in a glass of water, the marriage will be over.

Sugar daddies aren't for marrying.

6. The academic

Never marry an academic: while you're cooking the evening meal, hampered by a broken arm, coping with three measle-spattered children and an incontinent labrador, he'll be absentmindedly knocking his pipe out on your plaster cast as he looks for a place to sit and read. He'll forget birthdays, anniversaries – and sometimes even your name.

Never marry an academic.

In fact, hardly any men are good enough for you, but keep looking.

How to Meet Members of the Opposite Sex

Now that you have a rough idea of the type of partner you are seeking, you must make an effort to find him or her.

The following four methods have proved very popular, so make yourself look as attractive and interesting as possible and off you go.

1. The disco dance

Most people meet at dances, and discos are as good a place as any for establishing contact with the one you fancy. Once you have sighted your quarry, push your way confidently through the throng on the dance floor and chat up him or her as you dance.

It doesn't matter if you can't dance (no one would ever know nowadays), and if your chat-up line is a little dated or weak, never mind – your partner won't be able to hear you over the din, anyway. If, when the music stops, he or she walks off the floor with you, you've scored.

FANCY A ROUND OR TWO?

2. Join a club

This one almost always works if, for instance (and heaven forbid), you find yourself attracted to, say, the tennis type. What could be simpler than to join the club? If you do, you'll be surrounded by lots of them.

Chat up your chosen one, explaining that you've sprung a rib cartilage and can't play until your physio gives you the OK, by which time, of course, you're both up the aisle and all this sporting nonsense will have ended.

21

Delete where necessary

BEAUTIFUL/HANDSOME/UGLY/ACNE-RIDDLED/GENT/LADY/ whose interests include quilt-making/butterfly-collecting/bondage, wishes to meet person of the opposite/same sex. Object meaningful companionship/lust/heavy drinking/more bondage.

Ring 01-234 5678. If man/lady answers say you're a double-glazing rep.

3. Advertise

This is a very good way of checking what's on the market because you always get a picture of them before they see what you look like.

We at Duffer's Guides, ever eager to take some of the burden from your shoulders, offer the following typical advertisement.

Delete whatever does not apply and take it to your nearest evening paper. (Evening papers are always best — no one wants to think about this sort of thing first thing in the morning.)

4. Computer dating

This has become very popular over the last few years. Information about your interests, hobbies, etc. is fed into a computer which matches these details to those in its memory bank then offers names of potential partners with similar interests. All it *really* does is offer you the name of someone (like you) who is interested in computer dating – but the result is often successful, just the same.

How to Propose

No lady will ever admit to having proposed to her man. So the man must pretend that *he* has. With this in mind, we offer a few well-timed phrases for your guidance – though even as you utter them you should know that your girl's mother has already written her wedding invitations.

1. 'Darling, two can live as cheaply as one.'

Don't bother trying this one – she won't want to live cheaply, and she'll be off.

2. 'Darling, shall we pool our record collections . . . forever?'

This is a nice, heartstring-tugging one. It indicates a warm, giving nature.

3. 'Darling, I was thinking of opening a joint bank account with someone and I was wondering if you . . .'

This is a killer blow. She won't be able to refuse – no woman can say no to a man's money.

4. 'Darling, light of my life, what is life without you? Let me share your heart, let me be your protector, let me be your provider, let me show you love like you never dreamed possible. Be mine . . . forever. If you refuse me, I know I shall die.'

Don't try this one – she'll think you're mad.

5. 'Marry me now – before it begins to show.'

Direct and with the hint of a threat – this one usually works.

Getting Parents' Approval

The man should always ask the father of the lady he wishes to take as his bride for permission to marry.

Traditionally, the father was supposed to ensure that the suitor would be able to keep his daughter in a manner to which she had become accustomed.

Nowadays, the request is much more likely to be greeted with, 'At last! Thank God! I was beginning to think she'd be a millstone round my neck forever.'

But, even so, always ask – it's polite.

The man must always introduce his intended bride to his mother. This is to give his mother a chance to see whether her darling son would have done better with that little doll he'd been dating when last she saw him, and generally to check whether he's marrying beneath his station.

On the first meeting, therefore, we suggest your bride-to-be doesn't out-drink your mother before collapsing into her jam sponge. That sort of thing can often strain a mother-in-law/daughter-in-law relationship.

Don't worry about the father – for him anyone will do as long as it gets you living away from his booze cupboard.

Deciding upon the Day

Assuming there are no pressing physical reasons for haste, it's always a good thing to leave at least twelve months between deciding to get married and the actual wedding.

This is for three good reasons:

1. It gives the bride and groom time to plan the occasion.

2. It gives guests plenty of time to organize themselves.

3. It gives you enough time to get out of the country under an assumed name.

Getting married on a Friday or a Monday is considered to be very posh. However, the real reason for selecting such days is that many invited guests won't be able to take time off work, so you can keep the costs down.

So it's not posh, it's mercenary.

33

Always avoid Bank Holiday weekends. All your guests will be grumpy because they wanted to be away for the weekend and a church half full of people in tracksuits and sun-tops looks irreverent.

And try not to clash with big sporting events – rugby internationals, the Cup Final or the Grand National, for example. There's nothing worse than the organist interrupting the proceedings with cries of 'Lucky-Jim-by-a-short-head-at-sixteen-to-one'. It lowers the tone of things somehow.

34

Choosing the Ring

Now that you are to be married, you must choose the ring together, hand in hand. The same basic advice applies whether you are buying an engagement or a wedding ring.

1. Advice to the bride

From the lady's point of view, it's simple: go for the most expensive job you can con him into paying for. You must be practical about this. If the engagement doesn't work out, you should never, ever return the ring – you can always sell it. The same applies to the wedding ring. Get a nice big heavy one that can be melted down to make a flying duck for your neck chain.

2. Advice to the groom

The gentleman, however, should, on buying the ring, have already slipped the jeweller a tenner to lie about the cheap tray he proffers – quadrupling the price and romancing about the quality of the stones. It always works and your darling bride will never know (unless her finger turns green or she's only offered £2 when she tries to sell it to pay off heavy drinking bills in later life).

37

THEN THERE'S OUR THELMA'S SISTER'S BROTHER'S YOUNGEST.. AND HER HUBBY'S FAMILY...

The Guest List

As the bride's parents are responsible for paying for the wedding reception, they have the honour of preparing a guest list and sending out invitations to their darling daughter's wedding.

The list is usually made up in four sections:

bride's family and friends;

groom's family and friends;

bride's and groom's friends;

relatives you'd rather didn't come but can't leave out.

The list can be as long as the bride's mother wishes it to be or as short as the bride's father wishes it to be.

Invitations should be sent out early, to give your guests as much time as possible for them to think of good excuses for not attending – and for not buying the couple a present.

Where Shall We Hold the Wedding?

Together you must decide where you would like the wedding to take place.

Since most places preferred by men are not allowed to stage weddings, e.g. the back room at the King's Arms, the Boys' Bar at the golf club and so on, the options are not too many.

1. The cathedral

This is the scene of many grand weddings. Often the officials outnumber the guests. Also, if the bride should happen to arrive at the wrong door, she can spend ages looking for the guests, by which time most of them, overcome by cold and boredom, will have left.

Duffers should never get married in cathedrals.

YOU ARE HERE

2. The church

Most marriages take place in church, so it's no wonder churches have the whole thing off to a fine art.

Some can do thirty weddings a day without the rector breaking into a sweat or the organist repeating himself.

Rectors always get upset by guests throwing confetti in the churchyard. But if you really want to upset one, throw confetti at the couple as they're walking down the aisle.

3. The country chapel

This conjures up all sorts of romantic notions of an ivy-covered chapel, approached through a rosebud-bedecked lychgate by the lovely bride in white, and an enchanting service held by a minister who looks like Paul Newman.

In reality, half the guests won't be able to find the place; the bride will twist her ankle climbing in over a fallen wall; honeysuckle will bring on her hayfever; Paul Newman will forget about the whole thing and have to be brought in an hour late from the cowshed he's been mucking out.

4. The register office

Register office weddings are basic and clinical. Never invite a lot of guests to the register office. They won't all get in. And any marriage is liable to start off on the wrong foot if half-way through the ceremony you realize it's the bride's mother hammering on the door.

The Wedding-present List

It goes without saying that you are going to receive wedding presents, so you may as well be practical and ensure that you are given the sort of thing you want.

There's no point in receiving a dozen assorted breadbins and several sets of steak knives when you're both non-bread-eating vegetarians.

The secret is to make two lists, one headed 'Gifts' and the other headed 'Cheaper Gifts'. No self-respecting relatives or friends will want to have their name against the latter list, so you'll be quids in again.

THIS IS UNCLE BERT – THE ONE WHO GAVE US THE FLYING DUCKS...

Hiring Suits

Be very wary of people who work in suit-hire shops — they have a very vicious sense of humour.

Can the suit which fitted you (a slim 6-footer) so well in the shop be the same one that was carefully packed for you? Now you have it on, just before the wedding, you're sure it was intended for a 4-foot-6 orang-utang with a heavy dose of puppy fat. The top hat, too, is only propped up by your ears.

Always make sure your suit fits before the wedding day. All over the country during the wedding season suit-hire people are collapsing with mirth as they think of the chaos they've caused and the scenes of sartorial inelegance they've provided in the aisles of our churches and chapels.

45

The Stag Party

Most grooms have a stag party. It's a gathering of as many of his boozy friends as possible to celebrate his last night of freedom (until the Friday after he returns from his honeymoon).

The occasion will obviously be a very emotional one, as you will be able to tell by trying to engage him in conversation around midnight, by which time he'll be as emotional as a newt. That's when he'll be going on about what great mates he has. Of course he has – he's paying that night, so it's no wonder he has so many.

The Hen Party

The hen party is the female equivalent of the stag party. The giggling girls sit around the chosen pub, waiting for a Tarzan-style kissogram to arrive while they chat about weddings and babies – usually in that order. (Not-so-posh hen parties: reverse order.)

The already-married girls will offer cynical advice while the single girls long for the day when they, too, can be cynical as they merrily sip their way to closing time.

The Bridal Carriage

Some brides enjoy the luxury of a white Rolls-Royce or ribbon-festooned Daimler to transport them to their wedding venue. Others prefer the romantic charm of arriving by pony-and-trap.

Yet other brides have been known to arrive by tandem, but this isn't recommended; neither is arriving on a milk-float, even if Daddy is a tight-fisted milkman.

For the groom's part, it doesn't matter how he and the best man arrive at the church, as long as they're there before the bride. That's all that matters.

But remember one important thing: nothing looks worse than the groom and best man standing in the aisle, resplendent in their hired silver-grey morning suits, with bicycle clips showing.

The Bride's Bouquet

The bride's bouquet is one of the great attractions at a wedding. If it has been skilfully and artistically prepared, it will not only flatter the bride's colouring but will complement the bridesmaids' dresses and the flower arrangements that bedeck the church (at further cost to the groom).

Also, if the bride is in an 'interesting condition', any big bouquet will do to hide the fact.

After the wedding, brides often throw their bouquets to their bridesmaids. Legend has it that the one to catch it will become the next bride. Duffers, however, needn't bother with all that rubbish.

If you're getting married at one of those thirty-a-day churches, offer it at a knock-down price to the next bride waiting behind you.

49

The Wedding Day

1. The best man

The best man is the groom's right hand. He will have ensured that the bride-to-be has not found out about the various stripper kissograms that unexpectedly turned up at the several stag parties.

GREETINGS FROM ALL IN CELL BLOCK FOUR AND BIG LIL...

On the wedding day, he will help the groom to dress, checking for odd socks and that sort of thing, and get him to the church, more or less sober, on time. During the minutes before the bride arrives, the best man will hang on tightly to the groom, who by now will be thinking of doing a runner. He will also be in charge of the ring, which he will hand over at the right moment.

At the reception, he will act as M.C. and chairman of the proceedings. His big reward afterwards is to have the first chance to chat up the bridesmaids, but if you take heed of the advice that follows under the heading of 'Bridesmaids' your best man won't be too bothered about them.

2. The bridesmaids

Always pick ugly bridesmaids. There is nothing more devastating for the bride, who has taken three months to make herself look as good as she can, than to see all the male guests ogling the bridesmaids instead of her. So to make sure nothing spoils her day she should check through her friends, pick out a couple of real uglies and offer them the job.

Even if the ugly bridesmaids have stunning figures, she can overcome this by slipping the dressmaker a few quid to make the dresses baggy at the bust and hips.

Another good trick is to insist the bridesmaids wear dresses in a colour that clashes with their spots.

You're much better off with a little flower-girl or a page boy – ideally, a page boy who picks his nose.

FRIEND OF BRIDE OR GROOM, SIR, OR JUST A GATECRASHER?

3. The ushers

It's great fun being an usher. You usually offer this job to the brothers of the bride and groom. A properly organized usher can throw the whole church service into confusion by sitting guests of the bride with the groom's mob and vice versa. Another fun dodge is to find out who hates whom in the family and sit them next to each other – oh, and don't give everyone the right wedding service hymn sheets: shuffle in a few Christmas carol service sheets, which are always lying around churches. It's great listening to half the congregation singing 'The Lord Is My Shepherd' when the rest are singing 'Good King Wenceslas'.

A really good usher can liven up a dull wedding ceremony no end.

4. Confetti

As well as being guaranteed to upset clergymen, confetti-throwing is good fun, especially if you are on the throwing end. So why not be different? When your guests start slinging the stuff at you, the bride and groom, retaliate with your own cunningly-concealed boxes of confetti (which you've already dampened in the font so that it throws much more accurately – *and* it sticks).

Properly done, with bride and groom taking on all confetti-comers, opposing sides of the family will soon join in and good punch-ups should develop which you can enjoy from the safety of the back seat of your limousine as it purrs majestically away to the reception.

5. The wedding photographs

Forget what you hear about marriage being the joining-together of souls for the purposes of procreation and all that sort of thing. Marriage is to keep photographers above the breadline, along with vicars, organists, clothes-hire people etc.

You must book your photographer as well in advance of the wedding as possible to ensure you get an expert, not one with a secondhand disc camera and an old Polaroid who'll do the whole thing, prints and all, for a tenner.

An expert photographer can make the happy couple look like film stars and a soggy day appear like a glorious spring morn.

The album of treasured memories is a worth-while investment. There's something wonderful about watching the bride's father, a few years later, idly flicking through its pages, the tears gently rolling down his cheeks as he remembers what the whole day cost him.

55

The Reception

Immediately your wedding service has ended, you will want to hold a reception where the bride and groom can greet their guests together.

There are many styles of reception, from a sumptuous spread in a marquee-flanked hotel to having a few mates round for a quick Chinese.

You must decide on the type of thing that suits your situation best. Don't be put off by the bride's father asking for a small family get-together – he's biased: he's paying.

1. The posh 'do'

This is usually held in a five-star country hotel, at which four hundred elegantly dressed guests arrive to be served with champagne cocktails in a reception area banked high with flowers.

The whole party is then ushered into an impressive banqueting suite to partake of a carefully planned seven-course luncheon, each course accompanied by different fine wines, as indicated on the gold-embossed menu card. The toastmaster introduces the various speakers in well-modulated tones throughout the meal.

Later the cake will be cut – often by a ceremonial sword from the bride's father's or groom's regiment – and served with a mellow old port.

The numerous toasts are long and boring, but by now most of the guests have twigged that after each toast the wine waiter, who receives commission for each bottle drunk, will continue to fill the glasses indefinitely.

UNCLE ERNIE, FAMILY BORE

2. Stylish, but not over-expensive

Again, the reception will probably be held at an hotel. White wine reception on arrival, then take your seats as soon as possible for a nice four-course lunch (one bottle of wine between two couples).

The best man reads out telegrams at every opportunity in between proposing toasts.

The chopped-up wedding-cake is distributed to all assembled as the meal ends while everyone desperately tries to stop elderly members of the family from making more boring toasts.

3. The small, select dinner

This is usually held in a private room at a small country hotel where about a dozen friends and relatives are invited to dine with the bride and groom.

The whole occasion is very informal, usually with just one speech of welcome by the new husband on behalf of himself and his equally new wife.

It is always a very happy sort of gathering, with no one happier than the bride's father – he's saved a fortune by holding such a low-key affair.

SELWYN SMITH,
BRIDE'S FIRST
HUSBAND

4. The no-holds-barred family thrash

This is a jamboree to which everyone is invited – even relatives the bride and groom have never heard of, plus friends of any friends of anyone. A church hall is usually hired for such occasions, and liberally stocked with barrels of beer (sherry or shandy only for the women). At half past nine everyone goes to the nearby chippy, returning to knees-up the night away, so a piano is a must. This sort of thing is usually great fun. Everyone enjoys it except the bride and groom, who are expected to stay with the party until dawn.

5. The seating plan

Nothing will give you more satisfaction as you gaze upon the guests from your position on the bridal table than to see the chaos you've caused by careful arrangement of the seating. As a duffer, you may not realize how seating plans are decided upon. Well, it's like this.

You ensure that relatives who haven't exchanged a civil word for years are seated opposite each other on the same table. As for Uncle Bert, the chain-smoking, beer-swilling, disgusting-joke-teller of the family, put him next to Aunt Amelia, the teetotal, cigarette-hating family prude. (See, now you're getting the hang of it.) Put the golf bores next to golf-haters, and squeamish types next to the lady who wants to talk about nothing except her latest operation.

There are so many ways to ensure the reception is at least not boring. You may like to think of a few other ideas for your own family.

UNCLE TREV, FAMILY SLOB

61

Who Does What at the Reception

The guests are greeted by the bride and groom, the bride's parents and the groom's parents. This is done for two reasons:

(1) courteous hospitality;
(2) to check no gate-crashing relatives have crept in.

1. The best man

He will call upon someone to say Grace. He will also read all the greetings and messages from those not in attendance. If there are some greetings cards from people actually there, he should misread their names. It's all part of the fun of the day.

His speech will include a remark or two about how beautiful the bridesmaids look (he may as well lie a bit here – he doesn't want to upset everyone) and edited references to his experiences as a close pal of the groom's.

'MAY ALL YOUR TROUBLES BE LITTLE ONES' BEATS 'I'VE SHOT THE STORK' BY THIRTY TO TWENTY-EIGHT.

2. The bride's father

The bride's father is called upon by the best man to say a few words. He should say how sad he is to lose his lovely daughter (this starts the ladies crying) and how he can't think of anyone more worthy of her than her new husband (more tears), which may not have been what he said when he was sober earlier in the day, but should now come across with a certain conviction.

3. The groom's father

The father of the groom will welcome his new daughter-in-law into the family, and tell everyone what a wonderful wife he's sure she is going to make (this keeps the tears going). He then joins the bride's father and together they get maudlin.

4. The groom

The groom will thank everyone for everything – his wife for agreeing to marry him, her father for allowing him to marry her (in certain cases, for insisting on it), and so on.

To both mothers he will offer a bouquet of flowers while saying a few loving words about each (this really causes a deluge).

He may also like to give the bridesmaids a little gift to remind them of the occasion, which they will receive with surprised delight. This is when he says how he echoes the words of the best man about how beautifully they have graced the occasion (again 'milking the tears', as it's known in the trade: weddings are judged on how many tears the lady guests can shed).

A Day to Remember

If you have taken all the advice that we at Duffer's Guides have offered on previous pages, nothing can possibly go wrong and you will have a wonderful day.

The bride will turn up on time, looking radiant — her alcohol-fortified father slightly less so.

The best man has ensured the groom will be waiting for his bride (ideally in the same place at which the bride has arrived).

Whoever is officiating will do it beautifully. The hymns chosen will be most suitable and superbly sung.

Everyone will be enjoying your wonderful day — a day you will remember forever. Nothing can spoil it . . . it's yours forever. Enjoy every second of it; it goes far too quickly.

Understanding Wedding-Day Jargon

There is a language used at weddings that is not all it seems. Used usually by jealous relatives, the words thinly disguise catty remarks that would normally be made were it not such a wonderful occasion.

It's going to be a secret honeymoon.
She's not going to tell him
she's been there
the last three times.

I liked her dress.
I liked it, too, when
her sister wore it at hers.

Marriage is all about give and take, my dear.
If he doesn't give
you all his salary,
you take it.

She's done well for herself
. . . when you consider
some of the morons
she's been going out with.

**Don't they make a
handsome couple**
– apart from her,
that is.

**I've never seen her
looking lovelier**
– that heavy veil certainly
did the trick.

**I know they'll be happy
together.**
They've been happy enough
living together
for the past four years.

Marriage is all about trust and understanding.
You won't trust him
and he doesn't understand
you.

Her best friend introduced them, you know.
He was married to her
at the time.

She looked lovely in white.
White? Huh!
What a nerve!

I'd like to make a toast to the happy couple.
I fancy another drink.

Wasn't it a beautiful service?
It's not often the vicar is sober.

He's a very lucky man to have married her.
If his wife finds out, she'll kill him.

I understand it was love at second sight.
She didn't see his wallet at first.

She could have done better for herself
She could have married our Trevor.

The Wedding Night

There are many ways to approach the wedding night. They vary depending on the pre-wedded status of the happy couple (whether, for example, they've been living with each other, living on and off with each other, or are merely at the stage of 'Don't-you-dare-touch-me-until-we're-official, Ronald!', etc.).

The 'Let's-cut-the-cake-and-disappear' types

Normally, this healthy young couple have been living under separate roofs (owing to parental compulsion, not moral conviction). For them the wedding night will begin at about 5 pm and end with the sunrise – a week or so later when they have to get up to eat.

NO, NO! I **KNOW** WHAT TIME IT IS – WHAT DAY IS IT?

BRIDAL SUITE

The 'It's-supposed-to-be-the-best-night-of-our-lives-and-we-don't-intend-missing-a-moment-of-it' type of couple

This wedding night is normally for extroverts who have been living together since they were in college, so staying out of bed for one night is no great strain for them.

During the post-reception celebrations the bride will dance with all the male guests while the groom will be at the bar having what appears to be yet another stag night.

At sunrise they collapse exhausted on to their marriage bed, already strewn with the bodies of Uncle Hughie, good old Rupert and half the second XV, which tends to curtail any thoughts of amorous pursuits.

The 'Be-gentle-with-me. Mummy-told-me-all-men-are-insatiable-disgusting-brutes' type

This couple may be seen entering their honeymoon hotel nervously, she tearfully anxious as he signs the register, his trembling hand and sweating brow belying his assumed man-of-the-world pose.

Once in their hotel room, the sight of the bride in chocolate-brown winceyette pyjamas makes the groom wonder if it was worth putting on his Tarzan loincloth at all.

The last of the great romantics

Beware of being too romantic. It could ruin your wedding night. For example, take the groom who secretly arranges to have the bridal suite crammed with flowers: this has been known to bring on the bride's hayfever so that she starts sneezing and her eyes water, flushing mascara all over a face already moist from a running nose.

The chilled champagne arrives, brought by a leering, lecherous waiter whom you thump viciously, your bride becomes hysterical, and, after much consolation, she drops off to sleep, only to be woken by the strains of the gipsy violinist you hired in a romantic moment (before you realized he was tone deaf). She becomes hysterical again.

You seek solace in the champagne and eventually collapse in a drunken heap on the sofa, wishing you weren't such a romantic!

The experienced couple

Try not to show your partner that you consider the occasion to be just *another* wedding night. If you refuse to carry her across the threshold, saying 'The last time I did this, I put my disc out,' she might make awkward assumptions.

Neither should the bride say, 'Don't carry me across the threshold. The last couple of times I hit my head on the door-post.'

Comparisons, too, are irritating. Try not to say things like 'You're going to sleep already? Nigel would have been shouting "Geronimo" and diving off the top of the wardrobe for hours yet.'

The groom, for his part, should never say, 'I think I should warn you, my other wives complained that I was insatiable.' Nor should the bride counter with 'Was that it? Have you finished?' – or the even more wounding 'Have you started yet?'

Now that you have prepared yourselves for marriage by absorbing all our advice, may we at Duffer's Guides offer our congratulations to you both for what we know will be a lifetime of wedded bliss . . . a lifetime of love, an unending voyage of sharing and caring . . .

!

However, if it doesn't work out, we suggest you purchase *The Duffer's Guide to Getting Divorced.*